Ma

by Iain Gray

Lang**Syne**
PUBLISHING
WRITING *to* REMEMBER

Lang**Syne**

PUBLISHING

WRITING *to* REMEMBER

79 Main Street, Newtongrange,
Midlothian EH22 4NA
Tel: 0131 344 0414   Fax: 0845 075 6085
E-mail: info@lang-syne.co.uk
www.langsyneshop.co.uk

Design by Dorothy Meikle
Printed by Ricoh Print Scotland
© Lang Syne Publishers Ltd 2013

All rights reserved. No part of this publication may be reproduced, stored
or introduced into a retrieval system, or transmitted in any form or by any
means (electronic, mechanical, photocopying, recording or otherwise) without
the prior written permission of Lang Syne Publishers Ltd.

ISBN 978-1-85217-530-6

Matthews

MOTTO:
What God wills, will be
(and)
Every country is a home for a man.

CREST:
A lion's head, ducally crowned
(and)
A gold cross.

NAME variations include:
Mathew
Matthew
Mathewson

Chapter one:

The origins of popular surnames

by George Forbes and Iain Gray

***If you don't know where you came from, you won't know where you're going* is a frequently quoted observation and one that has a particular resonance today when there has been a marked upsurge in interest in genealogy, with increasing numbers of people curious to trace their family roots.**

Main sources for genealogical research include census returns and official records of births, marriages and deaths – and the key to unlocking the detail they contain is obviously a family surname, one that has been 'inherited' and passed from generation to generation.

No matter our station in life, we all have a surname – but it was not until about the middle of the fourteenth century that the practice of being identified by a particular surname became commonly established throughout the British Isles.

Previous to this, it was normal for a person to be identified through the use of only a forename.

But as population gradually increased and there were many more people with the same forename, surnames were adopted to distinguish one person, or community, from another.

Many common English surnames are patronymic in origin, meaning they stem from the forename of one's father – with 'Johnson,' for example, indicating 'son of John.'

It was the Normans, in the wake of their eleventh century conquest of Anglo-Saxon England, a pivotal moment in the nation's history, who first brought surnames into usage – although it was a gradual process.

For the Normans, these were names initially based on the title of their estates, local villages and chateaux in France to distinguish and identify these landholdings.

Such grand descriptions also helped enhance the prestige of these warlords and generally glorify their lofty positions high above the humble serfs slaving away below in the pecking order who had only single names, often with Biblical connotations as in Pierre and Jacques.

The only descriptive distinctions among the peasantry concerned their occupations, like 'Pierre the swineherd' or 'Jacques the ferryman.'

Roots of surnames that came into usage in England not only included Norman-French, but also Old French, Old Norse, Old English, Middle English, German, Latin, Greek, Hebrew and the Gaelic languages of the Celts.

The Normans themselves were originally Vikings, or 'Northmen', who raided, colonised and eventually settled down around the French coastline.

The had sailed up the Seine in their longboats in 900AD under their ferocious leader Rollo and ruled the roost in north eastern France before sailing over to conquer England in 1066 under Duke William of Normandy – better known to posterity as William the Conqueror, or King William I of England.

Granted lands in the newly-conquered England, some of their descendants later acquired territories in Wales, Scotland and Ireland – taking not only their own surnames, but also the practice of adopting a surname, with them.

But it was in England where Norman rule and custom first impacted, particularly in relation to the adoption of surnames.

This is reflected in the famous *Domesday Book*, a massive survey of much of England and Wales, ordered by William I, to determine who owned what, what it was worth and therefore how much they were liable to pay in taxes to the voracious Royal Exchequer.

Completed in 1086 and now held in the National Archives in Kew, London, 'Domesday' was an Old English word meaning 'Day of Judgement.'

This was because, in the words of one contemporary chronicler, "its decisions, like those of the Last Judgement, are unalterable."

It had been a requirement of all those English landholders – from the richest to the poorest – that they identify themselves for the purposes of the survey and for future reference by means of a surname.

This is why the *Domesday Book*, although written in Latin as was the practice for several centuries with both civic and ecclesiastical records, is an invaluable source for the early appearance of a wide range of English surnames.

Several of these names were coined in connection with occupations.

These include Baker and Smith, while Cooks, Chamberlains, Constables and Porters were to be found carrying out duties in large medieval households.

The church's influence can be found in names such as Bishop, Friar and Monk while the popular name of Bennett derives from the late fifth to mid-sixth century Saint Benedict, founder of the Benedictine order of monks.

The early medical profession is represented by Barber, while businessmen produced names that include Merchant and Sellers.

Down at the village watermill, the names that cropped up included Millar/Miller, Walker and Fuller, while other self-explanatory trades included Cooper, Tailor, Mason and Wright.

Even the scenery was utilised as in Moor, Hill, Wood and Forrest – while the hunt and the chase supplied names that include Hunter, Falconer, Fowler and Fox.

Colours are also a source of popular surnames, as in Black, Brown, Gray/Grey, Green and White, and would have denoted the colour of the clothing the person habitually wore or, apart from the obvious exception of 'Green', one's hair colouring or even complexion.

The surname Red developed into Reid, while

Blue was rare and no-one wanted to be associated with yellow.

Rather self-important individuals took surnames that include Goodman and Wiseman, while physical attributes crept into surnames such as Small and Little.

Many families proudly boast the heraldic device known as a Coat of Arms, as featured on our front cover.

The central motif of the Coat of Arms would originally have been what was borne on the shield of a warrior to distinguish himself from others on the battlefield.

Not featured on the Coat of Arms, but highlighted on page three, is the family motto and related crest – with the latter frequently different from the central motif.

Adding further variety to the rich cultural heritage that is represented by surnames is the appearance in recent times in lists of the 100 most common names found in England of ones that include Khan, Patel and Singh – names that have proud roots in the vast sub-continent of India.

Echoes of a far distant past can still be found in our surnames and they can be borne with pride in commemoration of our forebears.

Chapter two:

Celtic pedigree

Derived from the popular personal name 'Matthew', the surname 'Matthews', indicating 'son of Matthew', is of ancient Hebrew roots.

Meaning 'gift of Jehovah', or 'gift of God', it derives from the Hebrew personal name 'Mattathaigh', whose Latinised forms are 'Matheus' and 'Mattheus'.

Ranked at 95th in some lists of the 100 most common surnames in England, it is nevertheless particularly identified with Wales.

Although, in common with many other surnames, it was popularised in the wake of the Norman Conquest of 1066, some of those who would later adopt the name pre-date the arrival on British shores of invaders such as the Romans, Vikings, Anglo-Saxons and Normans.

This means that flowing through the veins of many bearers of the Matthews name today is the blood of the ancient Britons.

Of Celtic pedigree, these early inhabitants of the British Isles were settled for centuries from a line south of the River Forth in Scotland all the way down to the south coast of England and with a particular presence in Wales.

Speaking a Celtic language known as Brythonic, they boasted a glorious culture that flourished even after the Roman invasion of Britain in 43 AD and the subsequent consolidation of Roman power by about 84 AD.

With many of the original Britons absorbing aspects of Roman culture, they became 'Romano-British' – while still retaining their own proud Celtic heritage.

Following the withdrawal of the last Roman legions from Britain in 406, what is now modern-day Wales, or *Cymru*, fragmented into a number of independent kingdoms – with the most powerful king being recognised as overall ruler.

Recognised as King of the Britons, he had to battle with not only internal rivals but also the depredations of the wild sea rovers known as the Vikings, or Northmen.

There were also the Anglo-Saxons to contend with – as those Germanic tribes who invaded and settled in the south and east of the island of Britain from about the early fifth century were known.

These Anglo-Saxons were composed of the

Jutes, from the area of the Jutland Peninsula in modern Denmark, the Saxons from Lower Saxony, in modern Germany and the Angles from the Angeln area of Germany.

It was the Angles who gave the name 'Engla land', or 'Aengla land' – better known as 'England.'

The Anglo-Saxons held sway in what became England from approximately 550 to 1066, with the main kingdoms those of Sussex, Wessex, Northumbria, Mercia, Kent, East Anglia and Essex.

Whoever controlled the most powerful of these kingdoms was tacitly recognised as overall 'king' – one of the most noted being Alfred the Great, King of Wessex from 871 to 899.

The Anglo-Saxons, meanwhile, had usurped the power of the indigenous Britons, such as those found in Wales, and who referred to them as 'Saeson' or 'Saxones.'

It is from this that the Scottish Gaelic term for 'English people' of 'Sasannach' derives, the Irish Gaelic 'Sasanach' and the Welsh 'Saeson.'

The death knell of Anglo-Saxon supremacy and also what remained of Welsh independence was sounded with the Norman Conquest and the defeat of

Harold II, the last of the Anglo-Saxon monarchs, at the battle of Hastings.

Within an astonishingly short space of time, Norman manners, customs and law were imposed on England – laying the basis for what subsequently became established 'English' custom and practice.

In 1282, by which time most of Wales had come under Anglo-Norman rule, final rebellion against this was crushed by England's Edward I, and it is from this date that the heir apparent to the British throne has borne the title of Prince of Wales.

An abortive rebellion was led in the early fifteenth century by the freedom fighter Owain Glyndŵr, while in the following century, under Henry VIII, Wales was 'incorporated' into the English kingdom; in 1707, in common with Scotland, Wales became part of the United Kingdom.

Flourishing not only in their original heartland of Wales but also throughout the British Isles, bearers of the Matthews name feature prominently in the historical record.

Born in 1826 into a prominent Herefordshire family, Henry Matthews, 1st Viscount Llandaff, was the lawyer and Conservative Party politician known for his role in a sensational late nineteenth century divorce case that led to the ruin of a prominent Liberal Party politician. It was a case that rocked the establishment and one that today would give rise to lurid tabloid newspaper headlines.

Called to the bar in 1850 after being educated in both London and Paris, Matthews was made a Queen's Counsel in 1868.

He quickly gained a formidable reputation for his incisive examination of witnesses – a talent that was put to the test with great success in the 1885 court case involving Sir Charles Wentworth Dilke, 2nd Baronet.

Born in 1843, the Liberal politician had been elected Member of Parliament (MP) for Chelsea in 1868 and served as Under-Secretary of State for Foreign Affairs from 1880 to 1882, was admitted to the Privy Council in 1882 and, in the same year, appointed to the Cabinet as President of the Local Government Board.

His second marriage was to the art historian, feminist and trade unionist Emilia, Lady Dilke, while his younger brother Ashton Wentworth Dilke was married to Mary Eustace Smith, the eldest daughter of the Liberal politician and ship-owner Thomas Eustace Smith and his wife Ellen.

In a highly complex tale of adultery and infidelity, Sir Charles Dilke had begun an affair with Ellen Smith in 1884, the same year as his marriage to the unsuspecting Emilia.

The seeds of his spectacular fall from grace were sown in July of 1885 when his lover's youngest daughter, Virginia, claimed he had seduced her.

She claimed this had first occurred when she was aged 19, in 1882, and shortly after her marriage to the MP Donald Crawford. The affair is said to have continued for about two and a half years.

Crawford sued for divorce from Virginia in February of 1886 and the case was brought before the Honourable Mr Justice Butt.

Virginia Crawford did not appear in court, while Dilke refused to give evidence – and the judge subsequently delivered the rather bizarre judgement that while Virginia had been guilty of adultery with Dilke, there was no admissible evidence that he had been guilty of adultery with her.

Granting a *decree nisi*, dissolving the Crawford marriage, he also said he could see no case whatsoever against Dilke and dismissed him from the suit with costs.

But an investigative journalist, William

Stead, launched a public campaign against Dilke who, in a bid to clear his name sought to reopen the whole sordid case.

This was to prove his downfall.

In the subsequent trial he was subjected to a gruelling cross-examination by Henry Matthews, acting on behalf of Crawford, and the jury found that Virginia Crawford had indeed been telling the truth that she had been seduced by Dilke.

Evidence elicited by Matthews that proved particularly incriminating was that Dilke had physically cut out evidence of potentially embarrassing facts from his diaries.

Dilke, his reputation in tatters, was ruined and lost his Parliamentary seat shortly afterwards.

It was on the strength of his performance at the trial that, as Conservative MP for Birmingham East, Matthews was appointed Home Secretary in the Cabinet of Lord Salisbury – some sources asserting this had been at the insistence of Queen Victoria who had been impressed by him.

As Home Secretary, he served in the post during the gruesome 'Jack the Ripper' Whitechapel murders of 1881 to 1891; ennobled as Viscount Llandaff in 1895, he died eight years later.

Chapter three:

Science and invention

From politics and the law to the worlds of the sciences and invention, bearers of the Matthews name have also stamped a significant mark on the historical record.

A British marine geologist and geophysicist, Drummond Hoyle Matthews was a pioneering contributor to the theory of plate tectonics – involving variations in the properties of rocks forming on the ocean floor leading to what is known as 'seafloor spreading.'

Born in 1931 his work, along with that of fellow British geologist and geophysicist Fred Vine and the Canadian Lawrence Morley, is recognised as having played a crucial role in the development and acceptance by the scientific community of the theory of plate tectonics.

A research fellow at King's College, Cambridge and the recipient of the Geological Society of London's prestigious Wollaston Medal, he died in 1997.

Born in India in 1919, Paul Matthews was the

British theoretical physicist who headed the physics department of Imperial College, London and served for a time as chairman of the Nuclear Physics Board of the Science Research Council.

Also vice-chancellor of the University of Bath and a Fellow of the Royal Society and a recipient of the Rutherford Medal, he died in 1987.

Born in 1936 in Tulsa, Oklahoma, Gordon Matthews was the American inventor and businessman who founded the company that pioneered the commercialisation of voicemail.

Although it was first invented in 1976 by Stephen Boies of IBM, it was Matthews who three years later became the first to exploit it commercially.

Joining the U.S. Marine Corps as a pilot after graduating from the University of Tulsa in 1959, Matthews was first drawn to the challenge of attempting to 'mesh' human voices to technology after a fellow pilot was killed in a mid-air collision.

The accident, Matthews believed, had been caused by the pilot having to briefly take his eyes of the aircraft's controls in order to adjust his radio frequency.

Working for IBM, he helped to develop

voice-activated cockpit controls and, after a period with Texas Instruments founded his own company ECS Communications in 1979.

Partly based on Stephen Boies' original invention, Matthews submitted a patent for 'Voice Message Exchange', or voicemail, subsequently refining the technique with a further 35 patents.

Later changing the name of his company to VMX Inc., the first company to sell voicemail technology for corporate use, he died in 2002.

One particularly colourful and enigmatic bearer of the Matthews name was the British inventor Harry Grindell Matthews, who claimed to have invented that ultimate weapon of war – the death ray.

Born in 1880 in Winterbourne, Gloucestershire, he served during the Second Boer War of 1899 to 1902 with the South African Constabulary and was wounded twice.

Back in Britain, he claimed in 1911 to have invented an 'aerophone' device capable of transmitting messages between a ground station and an aeroplane from a distance of two miles.

Intrigued by this, the British War Office requested a demonstration – but Matthews demanded that no 'experts' be present and, when the observers began taking notes, he rapidly dismantled his equipment and declared the 'demonstration' to be at an end.

Although the War Office declared the demonstration to have been a complete failure, the colourfully extrovert Matthews proved popular with the Press, who rushed to his defence.

Shortly after the outbreak of the First World War in 1914, the War Office offered an award of £25,000 to anyone who could create a weapon capable of dealing with Germany's feared motorised air balloons known as Zeppelins.

First to rise to the challenge was the bold Matthews, who managed to demonstrate a remote controlled device, using selenium cells, against a remotely controlled boat in the Penn Pond in London's Richmond Park.

He was awarded the £25,000 but, for reasons that remain unclear, the War Office never took up the idea.

The inventor was in the public eye again in 1923 when he claimed to have invented a 'death ray' that could not only kill humans but also put electrical devices out of action.

He apparently demonstrated this to an overawed journalist by stopping a motorcycle engine from a distance.

Newspapers rushed into print with sensational accounts of the death ray, and in February of 1944 the War Office requested a demonstration.

In one such demonstration he did indeed successfully use a 'ray' to switch on a light bulb and cut off a motor, but the War Office remained unconvinced.

Matthews haughtily refused to give further demonstrations and instead threatened to sell his deadly invention to a foreign power.

Some inducements were offered for him not to do so, but he attempted to tout the idea to both France and the USA – until they, exasperated by his failure to provide convincing proof of his invention, in common with the War Office lost all interest.

Nevertheless still a magnet for wealthy private investors for other inventions that included the Sky Projector, capable of projecting pictures onto clouds, he was able to build a laboratory and private airfield at Tor Clawdd, in Betws, South Wales, where he had settled.

Later marrying the immensely wealthy

Polish-American opera singer and perfumist Ganna Walska, he died in 1941.

From science and invention to the highly competitive world of business, Sir Terence Matthews is the leading Welsh-Canadian hi-tech entrepreneur and business magnate born in 1943 in Newport, South Wales and Wales's first billionaire.

Immigrating to Canada as a young man after obtaining a degree in electronics from Swansea University, he still retains strong connections to the land of his birth.

With interests in a number of international companies that include Newbridge Networks and Mitel, of which he is chairman at the time of writing, he is also the owner of the Celtic Manor Resort Complex in Newport, near the South Wales coast, and which was host to golf's 2012 Ryder Cup.

The Celtic Manor Hotel, meanwhile, is the former maternity hospital where he was born; knighted in 2001, he is also the recipient of an OBE.

A multi-millionaire with a fortune estimated at £300m at the time of his death in 2010, Bernard Matthews was the British businessman who was a popular household name for many years.

Born in 1930 in Brooke, Norfolk, the son of

a car mechanic, it was in 1950 that he founded Bernard Matthews Farms Ltd., the Norfolk-based company known for farming turkey and producing turkey products.

The company launched its first television commercial, for Turkey Breast Roast, in 1980, and Matthews became famous for his catchphrase "Bootiful", delivered in a strong Norfolk accent, to describe the product.

Also known for his philanthropy and the recipient of a CBE, he was appointed a Commander of the Royal Victorian Order (CVO) four years before his death for his services to the Duke of Edinburgh's Award Scheme.

Chapter four:

On the world stage

An actor of stage and film for eighty years, Alfred Edward Matthews, better known as A.E. Matthews, was born in 1869 in Bridlington, Yorkshire.

Nicknamed "Matty", he first took to the stage in the silent era of films as a member of the British Actors Film Company, the production company that operated between 1916 and 1923.

A particular favourite with film-goers and known for his roles as a bad-tempered or rascally old man, his many screen credits include the 1943 *The Life and Death of Colonel Blimp*, the 1947 *The Ghosts of Berkeley Square*, the 1949 *Whisky Galore*, the 1956 *Around the World in Eighty Days*, the 1957 *Carry on Admiral* and, in the year of his death in 1960, *Inn for Trouble*.

The recipient of an OBE, his birthplace in Bridlington is recognised with a blue plaque.

On American shores, **Dakin Matthews**, born in Oakland, California in 1940, is the actor of stage, television and film who's many television credits include *Remington Steele*, *Dallas*, *Murder, She Wrote*, *NYPD Blue*, *Desperate Housewives* and *General Hospital*.

Big screen credits include the 1987 *Nuts*, the 1988 *Child's Play* and the 2000 *Thirteen Days*.

As a playwright and director and author of a number of scholarly works on Shakespeare, his 2003 adaptation of *Henry IV* won a Drama Desk Special Award.

Back on British shores, **Francis Matthews** is the film and television actor born in York in 1927.

Beginning his career with Leeds Repertory Theatre, his big screen credits include the 1958 *The Revenge of Frankenstein* and the 1965 *Rasputin, the Mad Monk*.

He is best known, however, for his British television role from 1969 to 1971 of the amateur sleuth Paul Temple in the series of the same name and adapted from the novels of Francis Durbridge.

As a voice actor, he also provided the voice of the puppet Captain Scarlet in the 1967 animated television series *Captain Scarlet and the Mysterons*.

Born in Nottingham in 1900, **Lester Matthews** was the English actor whose many screen credits include the 1931 *The Wickham Mystery*, the

1935 *The Raven*, the 1950 *Rogues of Sherwood Forest* and, from 1954, *Charge of the Lancers*; he died in 1975.

The heiress to the Hyatt Hotels fortune, Liesel Anne Pritzker is the American actress better known by her stage name of **Liesel Matthews**.

Born in 1984 in Chicago, Illinois into the wealthy Pritzker family, owners of Hyatt Hotels, her first screen credit came when she was aged 11 in *A Little Princess*.

She was nominated for an Academy Young Artists Award for Best Young Leading Actress in a Feature Film for this role, while other screen credits include the 1997 *Air Force One*, where she played the U.S. President's daughter, and the 2000 *Blast*.

On British television screens, **Sally Ann Matthews**, born in 1970 in Oldham, Lancashire is the actress best known for her roles in the soap *Coronation Street*, where she played Jenny Bradley, and *Emmerdale*, where she played Sandra Briggs.

Other television credits include *Prisoners Wives*, *Heartbeat*, *Where the Heart Is* and *Common as Muck*.

A favourite of British theatre and film audiences, **Jesse Matthews** was the actress, dancer and singer born in Soho, London, in 1907, the daughter of a fruit-and-vegetable seller.

Taking dancing lessons as a child, her stage debut came when she was aged 12 in *Bluebell in Fairyland* at the Metropolitan Music Hall, London.

Rising to fame through renditions of songs that include Noël Coward's *A Room with a View* and Cole Porter's *Let's Do It, Let's Fall In Love*, the number that became her personal theme song was the 1934 *Over My Shoulder*.

Her big screen credits include the 1932 *There Goes the Bride*, the 1934 *Evergreen* and, from 1978, *The Hound of the Baskervilles*.

Also known for her role during the 1960s as Mary Dale in the popular BBC radio soap *Mrs Dale's Diary* and the recipient of an OBE, she died in 1981.

Bearers of the Matthews name have also excelled in the highly competitive world of sport – not least on the football pitch.

Known as "The Magician" and "The Wizard of the Dribble", Stanley Matthews, honoured with a knighthood as **Sir Stanley Matthews**, was the legendary English player born in 1915 in Hanley, Stoke-on-Trent.

Earning 54 caps playing for the England

national team between 1934 and 1957, he played for Stoke City between 1932 and 1947 and again from 1961 to 1965.

It was while playing for Blackpool that in 1953 he became an FA cup winner in a final against Bolton that was dubbed "Matthews' Final."

He travelled around the world to coach young amateur footballers from 1965 to 1968. This included a visit to Soweto, South Africa and where, despite the nation's anti-apartheid laws, he set up an all-black team that became known as Stan's Men.

The recipient of a host of honours and awards that include European Footballer of the Year and induction into the English Football Hall of Fame, the teetotaller and vegetarian died in 2000 aged 85, while there are statues of him in the centre of his home town of Hanley and outside Stoke City's Britannia Stadium.

On the fields of contemporary European football, **Adam Matthews**, born in Swansea in 1992, is the talented Welsh right back who, after playing for Cardiff from 2009 to 2011, was signed for Scottish Premier League club Celtic.

Playing for the Wales Under-17 team from 2008 to 2009, followed by the Under-19 and Under-

21 teams, he has played for the Wales team since 2011.

In Australian Rules football, **Leigh Matthews**, nicknamed "Lethal Leigh", born in 1952 in Frankston, Victoria, is the former player who played for Hawthorn in the Victorian Football League in addition to coaching Collingwood and the Brisbane Lions.

A member of the All-Australian team in 1972 and an All-Australian team coach from 2000 to 2003, he has also been inducted as a "Legend" of the Australian Football Hall of Fame.

An inductee of the England Athletics Hall of Fame, **Ken Matthews**, born in 1934 in Birmingham, is the retired race walker who won the gold medal in the men's 20km walk at the 1964 Olympics; the recipient of an MBE, he also won the European title in 1962.

On the cricket pitch, **Austin Matthews**, born in 1904 in Penarth, Glamorgan was the cricketer who played for Northamptonshire, Glamorgan and the England national team.

An all-round sportsman – having represented Wales in the much different sport of table tennis and a talented rugby union player – he died in 1977.

From sport to music, **Cerys Matthews** is the Welsh singer, songwriter, broadcaster and author born in Cardiff in 1969.

First rising to fame as a member of the Welsh rock band Catatonia, formed in 1992, and enjoying hit albums that include *International Velvet* and *Equally Cursed and Blessed*, she has also performed and recorded with fellow Welsh singer Tom Jones.

In addition to being a successful recording star in her own right, she has also worked as a disc-jockey for BBC6 music and a documentary maker for BBC Radio 2.

In a different musical genre, **Edward Matthews**, born in 1904 and who died in 1954, was the African-American opera singer best known for his role of Jake the fisherman in the original 1935 production of George Gershwin's *Porgy and Bess*.

Born in Scunthorpe, Lincolnshire in 1946, Iain Matthew McDonald, better known as **Iain Matthews**, is the English singer and songwriter who, in addition to a successful solo career has also played with bands that include Fairport Convention – while his own band is Matthews Southern Comfort.

An inductee of the Country Music Hall of Fame, **Neal Matthew, Jr.**, was the American vocalist best known as a member of the country music back-up group – most notably for Elvis Presley – The Jordanaires; born in 1929 in Nashville, Tennessee, he died in 2000.

Awarded an OBE in 2011 for his services to music, **Colin Matthews** is the English classical music composer whose orchestral *Fourth Sonata* won the 1975 Scottish National Orchestra Ian Whyte Award.

Born in London in 1946, his many other noted compositions include his *Alphabicycle Order*, *Berceuse for Dresden* and *Night Rides* – while his many posts have included Prince Consort of Music at the Royal College of Music, London.

On Australian shores, **Patrick Matthews** is the former bass guitarist of the rock band The Vines, whose hit albums include the 2002 *Highly Evolved* and the 2004 *Winning Days*; born in Sydney in 1975, he became bass guitarist of the band Youth Group in 2004.

Born in 1888 in Braidwood, Illinois, **Artie Matthews** was the pianist and songwriter best known for ragtime music compositions that include his *Pastime Rags*; he died in 1958.

Bearers of the Matthews name have also excelled in the highly creative world of art and design.

Born in 1945 in Paulton, North Somerset, **Rodney Matthews** is the fantasy artist and illustrator best known for his highly distinctive work on album covers for bands that have included Magnum, Nazareth, Thin Lizzy, Diamond Head, Scorpions and Asia.

Specialising in postage stamp design, **Jeffrey Matthews** is the artist and designer whose first two stamps were issued in 1965 to mark the 20th anniversary of the United Nations.

Born in 1928, the veteran designer is a recipient of a number of honours and awards that include an MBE and, awarded in 2005, the Phillips Gold Medal for Stamp Design.